EDGE
BOOKS™

All
About
Dogs

BLOODHOUNDS

by Tammy Gagne

Consultant: Heather Whitcomb
President, Canadian Bloodhound Club;
Breeder of 2005 Eukanuba winner; Hall of Fame Breeder of
BIS/Champion/Working and Performance Bloodhounds

Capstone
press

HINSDALE PUBLIC LIBRARY
HINSDALE, IL 60521

Mankato, Minnesota

Edge Books are published by Capstone Press,
151 Good Counsel Drive, P.O. Box 669, Mankato, Minnesota 56002.
www.capstonepress.com

Library of Congress Cataloging-in-Publication Data
Gagne, Tammy.
     Bloodhounds / by Tammy Gagne.
     p. cm. — (Edge books. All about dogs)
     Includes bibliographical references and index.
     Summary: "Describes the history, physical features, temperament, and
care of the Bloodhound breed" — Provided by publisher.
     ISBN-13: 978-1-4296-2300-1 (hardcover)
     ISBN-10: 1-4296-2300-4 (hardcover)
     1. Bloodhound — Juvenile literature. I. Title. II. Series.
SF429.B6G34 2009
636.753'6 — dc22   2008026933

Editorial Credits
Jennifer Besel, editor; Veronica Bianchini, designer; Marcie Spence, photo researcher

Photo Credits: All photos by Capstone Press/Karon Dubke except:
Alamy/blickwinkel/Rainer, 16; Peter Greenhalgh, 12
AP Images/Alan Marler, 24
Cheryl A. Ertelt, 11 (top)
Corbis/The Art Archive, 9; Gaetano, cover
Getty Images Inc./Mark Raycroft/Minden Pictures, 7
iStockphoto/Luis Santana, 18

Capstone Press thanks Martha Diedrich for her assistance with this book.

1 2 3 4 5 6 14 13 12 11 10 09

Table of Contents

CHAPTER 1

SUPER SNIFFER

The sky is getting dark, and the air is getting cold. A little girl is lost in the woods. Fortunately, a bloodhound is hot on her scent trail. By sniffing the hat the girl left behind, the dog knows her scent. With its nose to the ground, the bloodhound follows the girl's path. Within minutes, the dog leads its police master to the missing child.

Bloodhounds are best known for their great sense of smell. These canine detectives make excellent search-and-rescue dogs. They can follow a scent that is hours old. Many people have been saved because of the great smelling talents of the bloodhound. Some bloodhounds also help police find criminals who have gone into hiding.

Bloodhounds have an excellent sense of smell.

EDGE FACT

A trail that a bloodhound has followed can be accepted as evidence in a court of law.

Is This Dog for You?

Not all bloodhounds work for the police. Many are kept as pets. Most bloodhounds are very loving. They like to give slobbery kisses to their human family members. These hounds are good with children. But some bloodhounds can be a bit stubborn.

If you don't like drool, this may not be the breed for you. Bloodhounds drool a lot. The slobber produced by a bloodhound can travel quite far when a dog shakes its head. Many owners keep towels around the house to help clean up the **saliva**.

Bloodhounds are loveable dogs, but they drool a lot.

saliva — the liquid in the mouth

If you decide that this breed is right for you, the best place to get a bloodhound puppy is from a breeder. Good breeders care about the health of their dogs. They'll be able to tell you about the puppies' needs and the food they eat. Breeders can also tell you about the puppies' personalities and which one would be a good match for you.

Many wonderful adult hounds also need to be adopted. Rescue groups take dogs that people can't care for and find new homes for them. If a bloodhound would fit into your family, a rescue dog might be a good choice. Whether you want a puppy or an adult, information is the key. Learn all you can about these dogs, and you'll be a good master to your pet.

CHAPTER 2

HISTORY OF THE BLOODHOUND

The bloodhound **breed** has a long history. Hounds with excellent scenting abilities were used by people more than 5,000 years ago. The bloodhounds we know today came from France. About 1,400 years ago, a French monk named Hubert bred the dogs. After his death, other monks continued Hubert's work. The dogs became known as St. Hubert's hounds. In some parts of Europe, people still call bloodhounds by that name.

St. Hubert's hounds were excellent hunting dogs. They could follow scents for long distances. Wealthy people in France and England prized the dogs for their scenting skills.

The breed was also prized because it had "pure" blood. That meant the dogs had never been crossed with other breeds. People often referred to the dogs as blooded hounds. Over time, the name was shortened to bloodhound.

breed — a certain kind of animal within an animal group

St. Hubert bred dogs that were good hunters.

For years, people used bloodhounds to hunt deer, bear, and other large game. But by the 1500s, bloodhounds had another use. Because of their great scenting abilities, police officers started using the dogs to find thieves and **poachers**. The bloodhound's nose surpassed those of all other breeds.

Even though the bloodhound had many talents, it slowly lost its popularity. In the 1800s, the population of large game animals decreased, and so did the need for most bloodhounds. Hunters needed faster, smaller dogs to hunt game like fox. Bloodhounds were bred with smaller dogs to create foxhounds, harriers, beagles, and other small dogs with good noses. Bloodhounds were used for hunting less and less. Even though they still did some police work, the population of bloodhounds quickly decreased.

Luckily, dog shows became popular in the mid-1800s. People bred bloodhounds to be used as show dogs. Some believe if the breed hadn't been taken to dog shows, bloodhounds would have become **extinct**.

poacher — **a person who hunts illegally**

extinct — **no longer living**

Dogs like the harrier (top) and the beagle (bottom) are in the same family as bloodhounds.

The white markings on some bloodhounds came from breeding with foxhounds.

The American Kennel Club (AKC) first recognized the bloodhound in 1885. But the breed's popularity grew slowly in the United States. People had to bring bloodhounds over from Europe, which was very expensive. A bloodhound from England could cost up to $5,000 — a huge amount of money at that time.

To Save the Breed

World War II (1939–1945) was a difficult time for the bloodhound breed. In Europe, people could not afford to keep dogs. Many dogs died because of a lack of food. Breeding almost completely stopped. After the war, breeders had to do something to save the dogs. They crossed bloodhounds with foxhounds. Foxhounds had been created from bloodhounds years before. The white markings found on some bloodhounds today may come from this crossbreeding.

CHAPTER 3

LOVING AND LOYAL

The first thing most people notice about a bloodhound is how sad it looks. Its droopy eyes, wrinkled face, and long ears make a bloodhound appear like it has lost its best friend. But nothing could be further from the truth. Most bloodhounds have cheerful personalities.

Physical Features

Bloodhounds are the largest dogs of the scent hound family. Adults usually stand between 23 and 27 inches (58 and 69 centimeters) tall. They weigh from 80 to 110 pounds (36 to 50 kilograms). Male dogs tend to be larger than females.

Bloodhounds might look sad, but they have happy personalities.

The bloodhound has a short coat. The coat may be black and tan, liver and tan, or red. Liver is a brown color that can vary from a dark chocolate color to light brown. There may also be a small amount of white on the dog's chest, feet, or tail.

Bloodhounds have long and narrow heads. When compared to its deep-set eyes, a bloodhound's brows look large. The dog's eyes are usually a color similar to its coat. Eye color can range from a deep brown to yellow.

The dog's long, soft ears hang low. A bloodhound's ears are actually very important to its excellent scenting skills. The long ears drag on the ground when the dog has its head down. The ears help gather scents.

Bloodhounds have helped the police find many missing people.

EDGE FACT

The most famous bloodhound is Nick Carter. Nick is credited with finding more than 600 criminals.

A bloodhound's skin is very thin and loose. It is soft to the touch. Folds of skin fall over the dog's forehead and neck. The skin folds near the dog's neck are called a dewlap.

But don't let all the skin fool you. Bloodhounds are very strong. Their necks are long and muscular. A strong neck helps the dogs track over long distances.

Scenting

Being a scent hound is a big part of a bloodhound's personality. People's noses have about 5 million **scent receptors**. The bloodhound has about 230 million. Bloodhounds can follow a scent for more than 50 miles (80 kilometers). They can even track a scent to the edge of a river, swim across the water, and pick up the scent on the opposite bank. Even if your bloodhound isn't a search-and-rescue dog, it will often want to take off on the trail of a great smell.

scent receptor — a cell in the nose that picks up smells

Temperament

Many people think bloodhounds are mean dogs. But that is simply not true. Purebred bloodhounds are tough, but loyal. They are also gentle. Bloodhounds can make good family pets because they are good with kids. But because of their large size, accidents can happen. It's important to watch children around these big dogs.

In the past, some hounds were bred to be mean and vicious. Many of those dogs were called bloodhounds too. Those hounds were used to track down runaway slaves in the 1800s. Because the hounds were so mean, people feared bloodhounds. Unfortunately, the two kinds of dogs are often confused. True bloodhounds are more likely to give kisses than bite.

EDGE FACT

Harriet Beecher Stowe wrote about bloodhounds chasing slaves in her famous novel, *Uncle Tom's Cabin*. The description in that book helped spread the myth that all bloodhounds are mean.

Bloodhounds are loyal
members of the family.

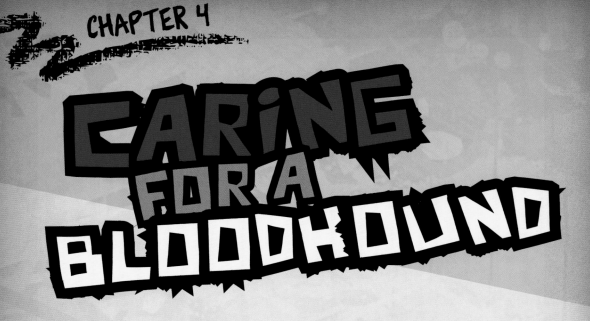

CHAPTER 4

CARING FOR A BLOODHOUND

Owning a bloodhound is a big responsibility. Owners must perform many tasks to keep their dogs in tip-top shape. Some jobs only need to be done weekly. Others must be completed daily.

Training a Pet

Because bloodhounds can be stubborn, early training is a must. If you don't teach your puppy how to walk on leash, it will pull you around the neighborhood when it is an adult. One way to start training your bloodhound is by taking it to school. **Obedience** classes called puppy kindergarten help owners teach their dogs basic commands. In most beginner programs, a puppy will learn to sit, stay, lie down, and come.

obedience — the act of obeying
rules and commands

It is a big responsibility to care for a dog this large.

Training for Tracking

This remarkable breed can follow a scent for several days. Even bloodhounds that do not work as trackers want to follow an interesting scent. But bloodhounds that do rescue work have to be taught how to do the job. People who train animals are called handlers. It can take a handler more than a year to properly train a bloodhound for search-and-rescue work.

Bloodhounds love chasing a scent.

Dogs do not have to work with police to put their scenting skills to the test. Bloodhounds can also compete in tracking and trailing events. These competitions offer dogs a chance to prove their abilities to follow a human scent. Tracking and trailing can be a great start for future work in search-and-rescue.

Daily Care

Like people, dogs must eat nutritious food to stay healthy and strong. Bloodhounds should eat at least twice each day. Dogs also need plenty of fresh drinking water.

Bloodhounds certainly don't need to be brushed and bathed as often as long-haired dogs. Still, some regular tasks must be done to keep this breed looking and feeling its best. Bloodhounds should be brushed about once a week. Brushing helps remove dirt and dead hair from their coats.

A bloodhound's ears must be cleaned at least once a week. This breed's long ear flaps hang down over the opening to the inner ear. The lack of air flow makes ear infections more likely.

Baths are only necessary when a bloodhound becomes especially dirty. Wrinkles, however, must be cleaned daily. Dirt can build up quickly in a bloodhound's skin folds. Owners must also remember to dry their dogs' wrinkles because bacteria grow best in moist places.

Finally, don't forget that exercise needs to be a part of a bloodhound's daily routine. Both puppies and adults need lots of exercise. Don't be surprised if you wear out before your dog does.

Brushing helps keep a bloodhound's coat clean and shiny.

Vet visits are important for keeping your dog healthy.

EDGE FACT

A healthy bloodhound will live seven to 10 years.

Vet Visits

The best way to stay on top of your bloodhound's health is regular visits with a veterinarian. At a checkup, the vet will weigh your bloodhound and take its temperature. The vet will also check the dog's joints and give it any necessary shots. You can ask the vet any questions you may have about your dog's care too.

Talk to your vet about bloat. Bloat is a condition in which the stomach fills with gas and then twists over. Bloat can cause death if it's not found in time. Talk to your vet about ways to prevent this problem.

Once your bloodhound is a few months old, it is smart to talk to your vet about spaying or neutering your pet. These simple operations prevent dogs from having puppies. The operations also help control the pet population.

Being a responsible bloodhound owner is a big job, but it has many rewards. Bloodhounds are celebrated for their amazing noses, but owners find their loving nature even more remarkable. A dog owner couldn't ask for a more faithful companion than the bloodhound.

Glossary

breed (BREED) — a certain kind of animal within an animal group; breed also means to mate and raise a certain kind of dog.

breeder (BREE-duhr) — someone who breeds and raises dogs or other animals

extinct (ik-STINGKT) — no longer living; an extinct animal is one whose kind has died out completely.

neuter (NOO-tur) — to operate on a male animal so it is unable to produce young

obedience (oh-BEE-dee-uhnss) — obeying rules and commands

poacher (POHCH-ur) — a person who hunts or fishes illegally

saliva (suh-LYE-vuh) — the clear liquid in the mouth

scent receptor (SENT ri-SEP-tuhr) — a cell in the nose that gathers smells

spay (SPAY) — to operate on a female animal so it is unable to produce young

Read More

Greenberg, Daniel A. *Wilderness Search Dogs*. Dog Heroes. New York: Bearport, 2005.

Perry, Phyllis Jean. *Sherlock Hounds: Our Heroic Search and Rescue Dogs*. New York: Mondo, 2007.

Internet Sites

FactHound offers a safe, fun way to find educator-approved Internet sites related to this book.

Here's what you do:

1. Visit *www.facthound.com*
2. Choose your grade level.
3. Begin your search.

This book's ID number is 9781429623001.

FactHound will fetch the best sites for you!

Index